WHY ARE YOU WAITING TO

EXHALE?

The Royal Candlelight Presents

Why Are You Waiting to Exhale?

A Devotional Cookbook
of
Recipes for Praising God in Everything

*Spiritual Gourmet Fine Dining Culinary Cuisines
for the
True Believer in God*

by Lynn Williams

Your Spiritual Gourmet Chef

Royal Candlelight Christian Publishing Company

"Royalty in the Making"

WHY ARE YOU WAITING TO EXHALE
When Everything that Has Breath Is Required to Praise the Lord?

Royal Candlelight Christian Publishing Company

Why Are You Waiting to Exhale?
© 2016 by Lynn Williams

Published by:
Royal Candlelight Christian Publishing Company
3855 Autumn View Circle NW
Acworth, Georgia 30101-7682
www.royalcandlelight.com
info@royalcandlelight.com

Email Address: royal.candlelight@hotmail.com
Internet TV Station Website: Ustream tv.com (Royal Candlelight)
Editor: Rachel Starr Thomson
Graphic & Media Arts Designer: Talon Williams
Book Interior Layout Designer: Lynn Williams
Sales & Marketing Director: Paul Williams
Social Media Strategist Director: Nichole Scales

Scripture quotations marked NASB was taken from The Hebrew-Greek Key Word Study Bible, New American Standard Bible, Revised Edition © 1984, 1990, 2008 by AMG International, Inc. These Scripture quotations marked NASB are from the *New American Standard Bible,* © 1960, 1962, 1963, 1968, 1971, 1972, 1973, 1975, 1977 by The Lockman Foundation. Used by permission.

Scripture quotations marked KJV are from the King James Version of the Bible. Public domain.

Scripture quotations marked CJB are from the Complete Jewish Bible. Brought to you by Messianic Jewish Publishers and Resources.

ALL RIGHTS RESERVED
No portion of this publication may be reproduced, stored in a retrieval system, or transmitted in any form or by any means—electronic, mechanical, photocopy, recording or any other except for brief quotations in printed reviews or articles, without the prior permission of the publisher.

Printed in the United States of America

Contents

Dedication	To Praise My Beloved Master Chef, Jesus Christ	5
Dedication	To Every Prince and Princess in the Kingdom of God	6
Foreword by	Johari J. Hodari, PhD	7
Introduction	Why Are You Waiting to Exhale?	9
Chapter 1	Everything that Has Breath Praise the Lord	16
Chapter 2	Becoming Instrumental in Your Praise	38
Chapter 3	Praising God at All Times in All Things	44
Chapter 4	Sing God a New Song of Praise Every Day	70
Chapter 5	Wisdom Is Found in the Praises of His People	80
Chapter 6	The Sinner's Prayer of Praise	90
Your Spiritual Gourmet Chef		101
RCCPC Advertisements		103

WHY ARE YOU WAITING TO EXHALE
When Everything that Has Breath Is Required to Praise the Lord?

Dedication to Praise My Beloved Master Chef, Jesus Christ

SPIRITUAL GOURMET ENTREE:

"Let everything that has breath praise the Lord. Praise the Lord."
—Psalm 150:6

Thank you, my beloved King, for allowing me to feast from Your blessed banquet table, where the precious Royal Candlelight, Jesus Christ, shines brightly on the spiritual meals prepared from the sweetest portions of spiritual food. As I dine, I am nourished and becoming a healthy princess. You are maturing me into walking worthy of the calling placed on my life in accordance with Your grace and mercy, and now I am equipped to assist You to serve as Your spiritual gourmet sous chef when serving up Your delicacies from the King's banquet table for all of Your princes and princesses to dine on. Praise You My Lord and King!

Love Your Princess
and
Spiritual Gourmet Sous Chef

Dedication to Every Prince and Princess in the Kingdom of God

From the Spiritual Gourmet Kitchen of Your Spiritual Gourmet Chef

PRAISE GOD

Dear Prince and Princess of the Royal Family of God, may you feast on all the PRAISES the Master Chef, JESUS, has prepared and placed in this Devotional Cookbook for your heart and mind to dine on so you can taste and see for yourself that God is

WORTHY of ALL PRAISES!

WHY ARE YOU WAITING TO EXHALE
When Everything that Has Breath Is Required to Praise the Lord?

FOREWORD

Lynn Williams has written an extraordinary book through the eyes of a culinary chef and a born-again believer in Christ; *"A person's gift clears his way and gives him access to the great"* Proverbs 18:16 (CJB). To incorporate your natural gifts and talents with your spiritual gifts is to fulfill your purpose here on earth. This book will inspire you to dig deep inwardly and encourage you to exhale while you are reading so that you can enter into perpetual praise and thanksgiving.

I have the privilege of personally knowing Lynn not just as a fellow author but as my sister-in-love (not law). I know her character and integrity as a woman of God.

Lynn has written several other books, such as *30 Minute Meals with God* and *The Royal Candlelight and You,* and her credibility on this subject stands alongside the other books that are successful in the Christian community. As you read this book you will find yourself connecting with its contents and will identify with it as well.

As you read this book you will look forward to your times of dining with God and the joy of experiencing His presence. The question, *Why Are You Waiting to Exhale?,* will arouse your innermost emotions. Why do I mention this? Because exhaling isn't always as easy as it seems. This book will share with you how to exhale at any time, be it winter, summer, spring, or fall. The insights inside this power-packed book will help you exhale praise and worship as much and as often as you desire.

As I read Lynn's book, I understood the necessity and the

freedom of exhaling and knowing who inhaled that breath into you. I am confident you will enjoy reading and exhaling too. Every page is crammed full of useful Scriptures and tips that you can profit from as you confidently exhale for the rest of your life.

Once you are endowed with what God has breathed into you during the seasons of your life, use the pages given in this book to pen it for a later time of reflection. And always remember, let everything that has breath praise the Lord!

This book matters to me, because I want you to experience the same fullness of exhaling in times like these as myself and others have experienced. Don't forget to *EXHALE*!

Johari J. Hodari, PhD
Fellow Author of *"There Is Something More"*
Newnan, Georgia

WHY ARE YOU WAITING TO EXHALE
When Everything that Has Breath Is Required to Praise the Lord?

Introduction

Why Are You Waiting To Exhale?

Prince and Princess

Scripture: Genesis 2:7
"Then the <u>LORD God</u> formed man of dust from the ground, and <u>breathed</u> into his nostrils the <u>breath of life</u>; and man became a <u>living being</u>." (NASB)

INTRODUCTION
From the Kitchen of Your Spiritual Gourmet Chef

WHY ARE YOU WAITING TO EXHALE?

Praising God for All His Goodness
"<u>Give thanks</u> to the L<small>ORD</small>, for He is <u>good</u>; for His lovingkindness is <u>everlasting</u>."— Psalm 136:1 (NASB)

To praise God is to exalt, extol, or glorify the Lord. Since God said to let everything that has breath praise the Lord, why is He having to wait for some of us to praise Him? It is for our good and God's glory! When you look at the very breath that was blown into mankind by God, you can see it was full of praise, because before we became a living soul, God spent His breath praising Himself. God praised Himself when He said that what He created was good, and at the end of the creation week, He said He saw that it was very good. The very breath that He used to praise Himself is the same breath He used to create everything, and it is the same breath He blew into us so that we might become living souls full of praise.

Praising the Lord is part of the process of you breathing properly. When you see how and why God breathed into you to make you a living soul, then you will understand why it is so important to praise the Lord. God inhaled praises into you as He exalted you to life, and He is just waiting for you to exhale praises to exalt Him in return.

Psalm 39:11b reveals that every man is a mere breath; therefore, you have enough breath in you to praise God with it! This breath you have inside you is the very breath of God's praises already within you. You were literally created with praise within you, and in order to continue your life in all of God's goodness with praise and thanksgiving, you are expected to exhale by praising God for your good, giving Him all the praises to glorify Him throughout your entire life. Praises are due to the Lord for all that He and He alone has done so that we may all exhale while we call on the Lord in praise and while we cry out to the Lord to make our supplications known to God.

Living with the Breath of Praise
"I cry <u>aloud</u> with my voice to the L<small>ORD</small>; I make <u>supplication</u> with my voice to the L<small>ORD</small>." —Psalm 142:1 (NASB)

You have great reason to praise God, because you became a living soul after your dusty life was spoken into existence. In the beginning God considered us all filthy rags, made from the dust of the ground. We were no different from the other creatures He created and brought forth on that same day, when they all became living after He spoke them into existence from the ground. Before the seven days in which everything was created, God said that the earth was formless, void, and full of deep darkness (see Genesis 1:2).

When you look at the dust we were created out of, you need to know that "formless" means *nothing, worthless/waste, vain/useless, bewildered/wilderness, desolation,* and *confusion/out of order;* "void" means *empty, invalid, and insignificant;* and this "darkness that is deep" means *misery, destruction, death, ignorance, sorrow,* and *wickedness.* This deep darkness is the fullness of evil found in the foundation of the whole world because it covered the entire surface of the earth. The Lord did not dig down and create humanity from the dirt, but from the top soil, which was the dust that had freedom to go when and where it pleased. Your will was created out of the dust, so you have the freedom to make choices and decisions to praise the Lord. It was the Lord's will to blow into our nostrils and cleansed us from all the unrighteousness found in darkness and from all the filth hidden from God due to fear found in the ground so that we could be formed in His spiritual image and likeness for all eternity. Now you and I have the breath of the Lord to cry out loud praises to His name without the spirit of fear because we received so much love from the Father, power from the word of the Lord and the sound mind of Christ from the Holy Spirit to know who to praise, how to praise, and when to praise the Lord at anytime and anywhere.

WHY ARE YOU WAITING TO EXHALE

When Everything that Has Breath Is Required to Praise the Lord?

Cleansed By a Breath to Praise the Lord

"O <u>sing</u> to the L<small>ORD</small> a new song, for He has <u>done wonderful</u> things, His right hand and His <u>holy</u> arm have gained the victory for Him. The L<small>ORD</small> has made <u>known</u> His <u>salvation</u>; He has revealed His <u>righteousness</u> in the sight of the <u>nations</u>." —Psalm 98:1–2 (NASB)

Like dust, we can show up anywhere at any time. We are free to move and to choose. Satan/beast, unlike us, came from the deeper dirt and was then covered in the very element he was created out of. And he, like dirt, doesn't have the freedom to move unless he gets permission to move against us. We can praise the Lord because we have always been on top of Satan, and now, according to Luke 10:19, we have permission to keep stepping on him! Satan is still nothing, worthless, and full of himself. He is vain, bewildered and confused as to who he is, because he thinks he's god, and that makes him totally deceived in all of his deceitful deception. He is insignificant because God said Satan is a liar, which means nothing he says is significant (important). He has no truth in him, and he can't produce life, only death, due to all the elements of the deep darkness from which he was created and which he was covered in. Satan is full of this same element of darkness, which was hidden due to the fear that was found in him, causing him to be a spiritual creature full of deep fear. This darkness was removed from us when God breathed His life into us, because God did not give us the spirit of fear, but of love, power, and a sound (disciplined) mind. In this way God replaced our original condition from the foundation of the world, but Satan was found to be flawed because he was not changed like we were.

Satan is afraid that we will find out the truth that he is fully evil due to deep darkness. He is nothing, worthless, vain, bewildered, confused, fully miserable, full of death and destruction, ignorant, sorrowful, and wicked. He has refused to bow down and give the Lord God praise, because he thinks he is god. He tries to exalt himself by getting us to respond to him in fear. He appears as an angel of light to get us to exalt, worship, and praise him, but he is only pretending to be something that he isn't. A true angel of the light is a divine messenger with a divine message of truth. Satan is a devil with a deception, a liar bringing a divination of lies.

Satan does not have the ability to change who he is or to alter his condition, but you have the power to make the right choices and decisions to change your condition and your ways, because you were created from nothing to be something else. When you breathe properly with the breath of life that God blew into you to make you a spirit like Him in all of His ways, you became His shadow to follow Him, to reflect His image, and to become Christ-like. You can imitate and display His likeness on the earth, shining brightly as the light of the world, because you have the Light of the Lord shining within you to reflect His glory

WHY ARE YOU WAITING TO EXHALE
When Everything that Has Breath Is Required to Praise the Lord?

and to give Him praises to be seen and heard as evidence throughout the world.

Satan was left in the elements of the ground based on his original condition; he never received the breath of God inhaled into him like mankind did. Mankind's physical life consists of all of the elements mentioned from the ground, but our spiritual life comes from the breath of life breathed into us. God is just waiting for us to exhale the praises that we inhaled from Him when He formed us into His own image and likeness. Our lives became spiritually meaningful and went from nothing to something else, from emptiness to a life that was worthy, useful, significant, orderly, full of light, mystery and purpose, alive, and peaceable, with the wisdom, knowledge, and understanding that fill us with love, joy and goodness for all eternity. God exalted us in this way. First Thessalonians 5:4–5 tells us, *"But you, brethren, are not in darkness, that the day should overtake you like a thief; for you are all sons of light and sons of day. We are not of night nor of darkness."* For this reason

Because...

Chapter 1

Everything that Has Breath Praise the Lord

Prince and Princess

Scripture: Psalm 150:6
"Let everything that has breath praise the LORD. Praise the LORD!" (NASB)

WHY ARE YOU WAITING TO EXHALE
When Everything that Has Breath Is Required to Praise the Lord?

EVERYTHING THAT HAS BREATH PRAISE THE LORD

God's Breath Was Used So Creation Would Praise the Lord

"For Thy <u>lovingkindness</u> is great above the <u>heavens</u>; and Thy <u>truth</u> reaches to the <u>skies</u>. Be exalted, O God, above the heavens; and Thy glory above all the <u>earth</u>."—Psalm 108:4–5 (NASB)

When you examine the Scriptures that give an account of everything God created, you will also see how everything was designed to praise God. Everything God created was praised by God first as He said "It is good." Therefore, the whole creation of God was invoked to praise the Lord from the beginning. We find in 1 Chronicles 16:31–36 that the heavens are glad and the earth rejoices, saying in their own ways that the Lord reigns. Another Scripture verifies this exaltation by telling us in Psalm 19:1–2 that *"the heavens are telling of the glory of God. And their expanse is declaring the work of His hands. Day to day pours forth speech. And night to night reveals knowledge."*

The Creation of Praises from Above

"Praise the LORD! Praise the LORD from the <u>heavens</u>; praise Him in the heights! Praise Him, all His <u>angels</u>; praise Him, all His <u>hosts</u>! Praise Him, <u>sun</u> and <u>moon</u>; praise Him, all stars of

light!* Praise Him, highest heavens, and the <u>waters</u> that are above the heavens! Let them praise the name of the L<small>ORD</small>. For He <u>commanded</u> and they were <u>created</u>!—*Psalm 148:1–5 (NASB)

Praise was to come from the heavens according to Psalm 148, and Psalm 89:5 confirms this when it states that the heavens received the breath of God through the Word of God when they were spoken into existence, and now the heavens will praise God's wonders because they know the faithfulness also of the assembly of the holy ones, who were predestined and designated by God to be holy. We were made in the image and likeness of God, who is the Only Holy One; therefore we are meant to be holy. The heavens express the heights of God's praise, which is coming from above from all those in heavenly places. This includes the angels and all the heavenly hosts, as we can see in Luke 2:13.

This is why in Psalm 148:3 we see praises coming from the highest heavens through the sun and the moon, along with the waters from above and the stars of light. They were all created to exalt God from above, just as the earth exalts Him from below. The heavens too were assigned to praise the name of the Lord. He commanded it, and they were created and established forever and ever to give Him praise. This was His decree, and it will not pass away, because God has said that His word will not return to Him void (empty, invalid or insignificant). The praise that was established in His creation from above will never end.

WHY ARE YOU WAITING TO EXHALE
When Everything that Has Breath Is Required to Praise the Lord?

As human beings, we were never created to praise and worship the sun, moon, stars, angels, heavenly host, or anything else God created above or below. Instead, like these things, we are to join in praise and worship the Creator of everything.

The Earth Is Full of Praise
"<u>Shout joyfully</u> to the L<small>ORD</small>, all the <u>earth</u>. <u>Serve</u> the L<small>ORD</small> with gladness; come before Him with joyful singing. Know that the LORD Himself is <u>God</u>;"—Psalm 100:1-2a (NASB)

The book of Psalms shouts joyfully with songs of praise that express the praises that come from everything moving on the earth below. The sea and all it contains are roaring joyful praises to God. Praises come from the sea monsters and the deeps, from the fire, hail, snow, clouds, and stormy winds. All are obeying and fulfilling His established Word. The mountains, hills, beasts, cattle, fish, creeping things, and flying creatures, along with the fields and all they contain, exalt the Lord. They all do their part to fill the earth with the praises of the Lord. Then you have the trees of the forest singing for joy before the Lord, giving thanks to His holy name for His goodness and His lovingkindness. They know that their praise and the glory they give God must be everlasting, since it blesses the Lord.

The earth was designed to constantly and consistently

praise God. It is filled with praises of joy due to the knowledge of God's glory. According to Psalm 97:1, *"The LORD reigns; let the earth rejoice; let the many islands be glad."*

Since God's creation on earth is already exhaling praises to Him because they joyfully know who the Lord is, then all of mankind—who are supposed to be the crown of God's glory on the earth and in all of His creation—should know that they are also expected to royally give praises to the Lord. Yet we seem to be holding our breath, waiting to exhale. It is for our good that we praise! *"For who is our hope or joy or crown of exultation? Is it not even you, in the presence of our Lord Jesus at His coming?"* (1 Thessalonians 2:19).

Isaiah was the prophet designated to inform us also that new songs of praise to the Lord should be sung from the ends of the earth, from those who go down to the sea, from all that is in the waters, from the islands, and from all who live in them. He too exalts the Lord by mentioning to us that the heavens are to sing for joy and shout out loud along with the mountains, the forests, and all the trees because of what the Lord has done to display His glory in heaven and on the earth. Isaiah instructs the heavens above and the earth beneath to burst into a song of the joy of their creation.

A Multitude of Praises from a Multitude of People
"__Praise__ the LORD, all __nations__; __laud__ Him, all peoples! For His

WHY ARE YOU WAITING TO EXHALE
When Everything that Has Breath Is Required to Praise the Lord?

__lovingkindness__ is great toward us, and the __truth__ of the L__ORD__ is __everlasting__. Praise the L__ORD__!"—Psalm 117:1–2 (NASB)

"Let the __peoples__ __praise__ Thee, O God; let all the __peoples__ __praise__ Thee. Let the __nations__ be glad and sing for joy; for Thou wilt __judge__ the peoples with __uprightness__, and __guide__ the nations on the earth. Selah. Let the peoples praise Thee, O God; let all the peoples praise Thee."—Psalm 67:3–5 (NASB)

Praises are expected to come naturally from all people from all nations, especially from those who are considered the holy nation of God, because dominion belongs to the Lord, and He rules with authority over the nations with praise and glory forever. As a holy nation, we are blessed by God. He said in Psalm 33:12 that *"Blessed is the nation whose God is the L__ORD__, the people whom He has chosen for His own inheritance."* Therefore, let us praise the Lord among the nations and sing praises to His name, because He has made us the head of nations and delivered us from the attacks of people who do not know to serve Him. He is the God who avenges us and subdues nations under us.

Peter repeats this praise in 1 Peter 2:9 to remind us that we are a chosen generation (or race of people), a royal priesthood, a holy nation, a people for God's own possession to proclaim the excellencies of the Lord who called us out of darkness into His marvelous light.

The breath of life that was blown into us is a breath full of holy praises, because we have been made in the likeness of God who is holy and has called us to be holy. We have received the mercies of God to enable us to abstain from fleshly lusts, which war against the soul (our spirit, heart, and mind) because of the love of God. We are not of the world, who are not praising the Lord, but we are *in* the world to let our light shine before men with the praises of excellent behavior and integrity. Peter says as we let our light shine in this way, in the very areas where the world slanders us as evildoers, they may on account of our good deeds glorify God in the day He visits them. When we live out the excellencies of the Lord before the world, they are able to see Him. These praises of good acts done as unto the Lord will even make our enemies to be at peace with us. When they see we have the peace of God and have become peacemakers, they will respond.

In Luke 19:37 we find that as the Lord approached the multitude of disciples near the Mount of Olives, they began to praise the Lord joyfully with a loud voice, blessing the King who comes in the name of the Lord to bring "peace from heaven and glory in the highest." They praised Him because of all the miracles they had seen. Therefore, we as God's modern-day disciples should begin to praise the Lord with a loud voice as well, for He is great and greatly to be praised for all of the miracles He has done before our very eyes—the healings, the deliverance, and our salvation itself.

WHY ARE YOU WAITING TO EXHALE
When Everything that Has Breath Is Required to Praise the Lord?

We are to bless our King and exalt His name forever and ever through all generations. In Psalm 145: 1-8 David states, *"I will extol Thee, my God, O King; and I will bless Thy name forever and ever. Every day I will bless Thee, and I will praise Thy name forever and ever. Great is the LORD, and highly to be praised; and His greatness is unsearchable. One generation shall praise Thy works to another, and shall declare Thy mighty acts. On the glorious splendor of Thy majesty, and on Thy wonderful works, I will meditate. And men shall speak of the power of Thine awesome acts; and I will tell of Thy greatness. They shall eagerly utter the memory of Thine abundant goodness, and shall shout joyfully of Thy righteousness. The LORD is gracious and merciful; slow to anger and great in lovingkindness."*

This is just a taste of the goodness of the Lord so you can see just how good God is. You need to keep reading to inhale the entirety of Psalm 145. This beautiful psalm will give you a mouth full of praise so you can keep breathing properly with the breath designed to inhale all of God's greatness and exhale the sweet taste of all His praises. His greatness is for your good and His glory. As His disciples, we are to spread this good news throughout our lifetime for all who have eyes to see and ears to hear so they may see, hear, and experience for themselves the goodness of the Lord. They may taste and see of His goodness, for He is the Rock of Ages.

Your Praise Is as Solid as a Rock
"Blessed be the LORD, my rock."—Psalm 144:1

Your praises should be as solid as a rock. Scripture expresses in Psalm 118:22 that our God is the Chief Cornerstone who was rejected by the builders, but we stand on this Rock with praise because it is our solid foundation. We are blessed to build our lives on God, and He is marvelous in our eyes. We have been blessed from the house of the Lord, which is built to hold a multitude of praises as we worship the Lord and shout out holy praises on the earth. We are the house of God on earth; we are the temple built to declare that the Lord is holy and that He is the head of church and of everything. We gather together under His roof to hear a word from the Lord our God and to bless, edify, and glorify His Holy Name.

If we are silent, if we don't want to praise God for all of His goodness and greatness according to Luke 19:40, then the rocks will cry out praises to the Rock. If we do not do it, the stones will let Him know there is no Rock like our God and no one holy like the Lord, who can make peace by whispering a word of silence to rebuke and bind anyone or anything that comes against us to cause a disturbance and keep us from praising Him in everything we are experiencing in life.

Deuteronomy 32:30 states that if we are silent, it is because *"you have deserted the Rock, who fathered you; you forgot the*

WHY ARE YOU WAITING TO EXHALE
When Everything that Has Breath Is Required to Praise the Lord?

God who gave you birth." Instead of holding your breath and waiting in silence to exhale, God expects you to exhale like Samuel exhaled in 2 Samuel 22:2-3; *"And he said, 'The LORD is my rock, and my fortress, and my deliverer; My God, my rock, in whom I take refuge; my shield and the horn of my salvation, my stronghold and my refuge; My savior, Thou dost save me from violence.'"* This praise comes from the breath of one who knows that the Lord is their Provider and Protector and that they have no rock except our God. Both Psalm 18:46 and 2 Samuel 22:47 express this well: *"Praise be to my Rock! Exalted be my God, the Rock, my Savior!"* We can always exhale this praise, repeating these words for ourselves. Psalm 71:3 allows us to inhale the truth that the Lord can *"be my rock of refuge, to which I can always go; give the command to save me, for you are my rock and my fortress."*

We must remember not to be silent, not to hold our breath of praise. After all, we want God to respond to us and not hold His breath where we are concerned. We do not want Him to be silent when we need Him to speak a word on our behalf or invoke vengeance upon our adversaries.

Psalm 28:1–4 states this well: *"To Thee, O LORD, I call; My rock, do not be deaf to me, lest if Thou be silent to me, I become like those who go down to the pit. Hear the voice of my supplications when I cry to Thee for help, when I lift up my hands toward Thy holy sanctuary. Do not drag me away with the wicked and with those who work iniquity; who speak peace with their neighbors, while evil is in their hearts. Requite them according to their work and according to the evil of their practices; Requite them according to the deeds of their hands; repay them their recompense."*

God can use His breath to speak to the wicked and to all those with deceitful mouths of destruction, who speak against you with lying tongues and surround you with hatred. At times in life people will fight against us without cause and repay us with evil when we have done nothing but good to them. They will exchange their hatred for our love. In these times, we can pray like it instructs us to do in Psalm 109:1, because the Lord is the God of our praise and can change that which was meant for evil and turn it around for our good. Psalm 28:6–7 expresses it this way: *"Praise be to the LORD, for he has heard my cry for mercy. The LORD is my strength and my shield; my heart trusts in him, and he helps me. My heart leaps for joy, and with my song I praise him."*

Our praises and supplication to the Lord give us victory, because praise gives us the help needed to tread down our adversaries. Psalm 31:1–4 can become our testimony: *"In thee, O LORD, I have taken refuge; let me never be ashamed; in thy righteousness deliver me. Incline thine ear to me, rescue me*

WHY ARE YOU WAITING TO EXHALE
When Everything that Has Breath Is Required to Praise the Lord?

quickly; be thou to me a rock of strength, a stronghold to save me. For thou art my rock and my fortress; for thy name's sake thou wilt lead me and guide me. Thou wilt pull me out of the net which they have secretly laid for me; for thou art my strength."

You can breathe easier knowing that the Lord has a breath that is so strong that when He speaks to your heart and mind to remind you to place your trust in Him, His words will become your strong tower. You can inhale the breath of those words to ease your troubled heart and mind.

Taking a Deep Breath to Praise the Lord

"It is good to give thanks to the Lord, and to sing praises to Thy name, O Most High; to declare Thy lovingkindness in the morning, and Thy faithfulness by night."—Psalm 92:1–2 (NASB)

We should take deep breaths of praise to give thanks to the Lord from morning to night. Doing this shows that you have a strong heart for the Lord, because you love God with all of your heart as He has commanded, and you carry out your love through obedience. To praise continually you must have a heart that is steadfast and can sing praises all day long, even with your soul and mind, according to Psalm 108:1, because in spite of all the evil surrounding you and coming against you, you know for yourself that the faithfulness of God's loving-kindness covers you all day and all night. He will do you no harm, but His faithfulness and loving-kindness are to give you a future and a hope. Therefore, we must keep our minds stayed on the love and faithfulness of Jesus Christ with praise so that we may receive perfect peace.

You can awake with your heart and mind stayed on Jesus. You can awaken with spiritual singing, giving thanks to the Lord as you come into His courts of praise, bringing your petitions and supplications to the Lord with thanksgiving because you love Him and know that He hears your voice. Your requests are made known to Him even before you ask.

By noon, your heart should still be beating strong with deep praises as you labor in the love of God to do that which is according to His will. You can praise Him at midday as He orders your steps, to guide you and provide you with the counsel needed to walk worthy of your calling through the Holy Spirit.

By evening, keep breathing deeply with praises as you meet the King at the banquet table to feast on the bread of life and drink the wine of the Holy Spirit to quench all your thirst to do the will of God. Over you is a banner of love as the King serves you with love and kindness through His Word. Make a reservation for two to dine on the Word every night. Spend time studying the Word as it comes from the breath of the Lord so you can learn how to praise Him from the depths of your heart as He continues to reveal Himself to you. Discuss your concerns regarding your life with

WHY ARE YOU WAITING TO EXHALE
When Everything that Has Breath Is Required to Praise the Lord?

Him and ask about the concerns He has on His heart for you. Ask, seek, and find Him to be generous and to be just who He says He is in all of His glory.

By night you can lie down for a peaceful night's sleep, knowing that you can rest assured in His praises. You can rest knowing that He will watch over you, holding you in the security of His loving arms of protection. As you dined with the King, you received the peace of God that surpasses all understanding. As you sleep, your spirit can deeply meditate with praise and worship on all God's doings and be amazed at the works of His hands. All day you will have experienced the Lord and His wonderful works, because you have come to know through your continual praise and worship that He is your Intercessor who has interceded on your behalf. The Most High God is your fortress and stronghold, and He keeps those in perfect peace whose minds are stayed on Him.

You can praise the Lord because He is your shield and refuge in times of trouble and has delivered you from all dangers seen and unseen. You can praise God, because you have allowed Him to lead and guide you. He has rescued you from all your enemies, as His Word expresses in Psalm 18:1–3 and Psalm 143:5. Psalm 139:1–3 testifies that the Lord searches you and knows you personally. He knows when you sit down and when you rise up, as well as knowing your thoughts from afar. He has scrutinized your path and your lying down. He has an art of praise that is intimately acquainted with all your ways, even before there is a word on your tongue, because He knows all things. Therefore, praise God in advance, for He has revealed to you that He is omnipresent and omniscient: He knows all, sees all, and is everywhere at all times, searching our hearts and minds to hear our praises.

When you exhale praises to God from the meditation of your heart in your secret times with Him, they are pleasing in God's sight. They give evidence of your faith in Christ and openly show your gratitude to God for being your Rock and your Redeemer. The Most High God is God the Father, God the Son, and God the Holy Spirit, and these Three being One God deserve the highest praise—the continual *hallelujah* that comes from our hearts and minds.

We can give thanks to the Lord with a pure heart and a sound mind of thanksgiving. We can enter His courts with great praise for all of His goodness. Psalm 111:7–9 tells us the Lord's works are truth and justice; his precepts (commandments/spiritual instructions) are sure, and they are upheld forever and ever. God's works are performed in the truth and uprightness of His heart and mind. He sent redemption through His Son, the Lord God, to His people, and He has ordained His covenant with us for all eternity.

The Most High God deserve the highest praise! This is simply because there is no one equal to or above Him, since the

WHY ARE YOU WAITING TO EXHALE
When Everything that Has Breath Is Required to Praise the Lord?

Lord is the Creator and the Possessor of heaven and earth and all that dwells therein. All praises go to the Lord, who deserves the highest praise. Isaiah 42:5 reveals who our God is: *"The Creator of the heavens, who stretches them out, who spreads out the earth with all that springs from it, who gives breath to its people, and life to those who walk on it."* He is the One who deserves praise that is above all praises!

Giving God the Breath of Your Highest Praise
*"Great is the L*ORD*, and <u>highly</u> to be <u>praised</u>; and His greatness is <u>unsearchable</u>."—Psalm 145:3 (NASB)*

We exhale *hallelujah* to the Lord for His unsearchable greatness, for where there are two or three gathered in the name of the Lord, there God is in our midst, dwelling in our praises. The Two (God the Son and God the Holy Spirit) or Three (the Most High God in His fullness) gather in the Name, and the Lord will dwell within us because this is the God who is in the midst of us, indwelling our praises. Shout *hallelujah* out loud, because this expresses the great trust that you have in the Lord as you sing praises that express His greatness. Rejoice in your heart while you build a strong foundation of solid praise on the Rock of your salvation, cementing it with trust in your heart.

When you exhale your greatest praises and the Most High

God dwells in the midst of your praise, then the gates of hell will not prevail. The enemy will not overcome you, because greater is the Most High God that is in you than Satan, who is in the world trying to come against you. With every temptation he brings against you, Satan wants to stop you from pleasing God with your praises. His hope is that God will not be in the midst of you so he can attack every area of your life.

Therefore, we must praise God in spite of our circumstances! We must praise Him in the midst of loneliness and distressing circumstances, because in doing so, we ensure that no weapon Satan can form against us will prosper. Since "prosper" here means to gain advantage, we know that Satan cannot spiritually gain any advantage in trying to separate us from God in the midst of our troubles, because as long as we keep praising God, God is in the midst of our praise. He will assist us in overcoming and stop Satan from succeeding in his attempts to try to spiritually kill, steal, or destroy your intimate relationship with God.

Satan is a defeated foe, because God will never leave you alone nor forsake (neglect) you. Even when you feel that you are all alone in this world, left to come against your adversary on your own, God will not neglect you. He has said that this battle is not yours, but His. So we can continue to praise God through every battle fought, and we will win with great victory against our enemy.

WHY ARE YOU WAITING TO EXHALE
When Everything that Has Breath Is Required to Praise the Lord?

If Satan were to succeed in spiritually killing, stealing from, or destroying you, causing a spiritual separation from God, you would not be able to praise God, and God would then receive no glory from your life. The psalms tell us that the dead can't praise the Lord. Therefore, you must guard your heart and mind by remembering to praise God during your trials and tribulations, especially during spiritual attacks from your enemy, Satan. As you continually praise, it will remind you—and let everyone and everything else know!—that you're still alive in Christ. During every situation that looks hopeless, God is with you. He hasn't left you during any of your situations or circumstances. Therefore, you can praise God with everything that is within you. In times of trouble, you have the greatest ability to . . .

PERSONALLY PRAISE GOD
WITH EVERY BREATH THAT IS EXHALED
FROM THE
GREATNESS THAT'S WITHIN YOU

Scripture: Psalm 103:1
"<u>Bless</u> the LORD, O my <u>soul</u>; and all that is <u>within</u> me, bless His <u>holy</u> name!" (NASB)

WHY ARE YOU WAITING TO EXHALE
When Everything that Has Breath Is Required to Praise the Lord?

Personal Praises Exhaled from Your Breath

Write down a list of situations or circumstances that you are presently experiencing.

_____
_____
_____
_____
_____
_____
_____
_____
_____
_____
_____
_____
_____
_____
_____
_____
_____
_____
_____
_____
_____
_____

Write down a list of Scriptures you have received from the breath of Lord. List the Scriptures He has given you to inhale. He will help you to breathe and show the greatness within you during these situations or circumstances that you are presently experiencing.

_____
_____
_____
_____
_____
_____
_____
_____
_____
_____
_____
_____
_____
_____
_____
_____
_____
_____
_____
_____

WHY ARE YOU WAITING TO EXHALE
When Everything that Has Breath Is Required to Praise the Lord?

Write down praises to sing to the Lord to give Him evidence (both seen and heard) of your trust in Him based on what you have inhaled from His Word. The Lord has said that He will bless you with greatness, but now you must exhale your breath of praise to bless the Lord. His Word that you inhale has given you life and will keep you alive and holy in these situations and circumstances.

_____
_____
_____
_____
_____
_____
_____
_____
_____
_____
_____
_____
_____
_____
_____
_____
_____
_____
_____
_____
_____
_____
_____

Chapter 2

Becoming Instrumental in Your Praise

Prince and Princess

Scripture: 2 Chronicles 5:13
"...In unison when the trumpeters and the singers were to make themselves heard with one voice to <u>praise</u> and to glorify the LORD, and when they lifted up their voice accompanied by trumpet and cymbals and instruments of music, and when they <u>praised</u> the LORD saying, 'He indeed is <u>good</u> for His lovingkindness is everlasting, the house of the LORD was filled with a <u>cloud</u>, so that the priests could not stand to minister because of the cloud, for the <u>glory</u> of the LORD filled the house of God."

Scripture: Isaiah 38:20
"The LORD will surely <u>save</u> me; so we will play my <u>songs</u> on <u>stringed instruments</u> all the days of our life at the house of the LORD."

WHY ARE YOU WAITING TO EXHALE
When Everything that Has Breath Is Required to Praise the Lord?

BECOMING INSTRUMENTAL IN YOUR PRAISE

Making Music with the Instruments of Praise

"Sing for joy in the L<small>ORD</small>, O you <u>righteous</u> ones; <u>praise</u> is <u>becoming</u> to the <u>upright</u>. <u>Give</u> <u>thanks</u> to the L<small>ORD</small> with the lyre; <u>sing praises</u> to Him with a harp of ten strings. <u>Sing</u> to Him a new song; play <u>skillfully</u> with a shout of joy. For the <u>word</u> of the L<small>ORD</small> is <u>upright</u>; and all of His work is done in <u>faithfulness</u>."—Psalm 33:1–4 (NASB)

We give praise to the Creator and Preserver of life with instruments of praise so that all inhabitants of the world may stand in awe of Him. The Lord looks down from His dwelling place in heaven to see all the sons of men and listen to the beautiful music that comes from the hearts of those who praise Him with instruments of praise.

The Scriptures mention many musical instruments of praise. Praise comes from the blowing of the trumpet in Psalm 150:3. Joy flows from timbrels and sweet sounds from harps and lyres as worshippers skillfully make music and play their new songs to the Lord with shouts of joy. Psalm 150:4–5 speaks of stringed instruments, pipes, and resounding cymbals praising God out loud to let everyone know that everything that has breath should praise the Lord!

Whether or not you can physically play an instrument, you have a built-in instrument called your vocal cords, which you can use to play a heart song of praises at any time. You can serenade God anywhere with your songs of praise and create beautiful music through the set of pipes you have within. Your song can accompany your heart. It will be pleasing to the ear of God when you exhale your exaltation and praise songs through your vocal cords in an audible song.

Because we are equipped with an instrument, we have the opportunity to fill our spiritual temples with praise to the Lord to enjoy while He dwells within us. He gets to enjoy the melody of a joyful sound from your heart that beats in tune with His heart of love and gladness. Sing out the love you have for Him and for others as you sing to the Lord your love songs of praise for all to hear. He will be glad!

Our songs of love sound sweet to the Lord because we have not become a noisy gong or a clanging cymbal like that mentioned in 1 Corinthians 13:1, but rather our songs are written with words of love. We are fully known by God as we abide in faith, hope, and love. The greatest of these is love, because we have received the greatest love through our faith in Christ who loved us from the beginning of life.

WHY ARE YOU WAITING TO EXHALE
When Everything that Has Breath Is Required to Praise the Lord?

The Sweet Melody of a Heart full of Praise Comes from a Breath that Is Blessed

"How <u>blessed</u> are those whose <u>way</u> is <u>blameless</u>, who walk in the <u>law</u> of the L<small>ORD</small>. *How blessed are those who <u>observe</u> His testimonies, who seek Him with all their <u>heart</u>. —Psalm 119:1–2 (NASB)*

Just like God's people in the Old Testament dedicated their instruments to the Lord, we too can dedicate our voices to praising the Lord with a festival of great rejoicing. The Levites and priests praised the Lord every day with resounding instruments that were dedicated to the Lord. We as His holy priesthood can dedicate our praises as we dedicate our lives to praising the Lord every day. As we praise Him each and every day, we offer sacrifices of praise with the sounds of joyful shouting in the tents of the righteous, like it was expressed in Psalm 118:15. We shout and sing from the joy of our salvation. This is our reasonable service to the Lord as we serve Him with gladness, praising with the breath of life as He inhales and we exhale.

In return we find the Lord doing the same thing. First Thessalonians 4:16 says in regard to those who have died in Christ, *"For the Lord Himself will descend from heaven with a shout, with the voice of the archangel, and with the trumpet of God; and the dead in Christ shall rise first."*

Your songs of praise are coming from your heartstrings, because you know that *"The LORD will save me, and we will sing with stringed instruments all the days of our lives in the temple of the LORD"* (Isaiah 38:20). Be the first to rise and give God the honor due Him because you should be . . .

In Tune with the Lord to Continue Breathing with Praise

What have you learned about the heart of God? You can tune your heartstrings to play the same notes as you make melodies through your vocal cords, serenading the Lord with new songs. Write down what you have learned about God's heart.

_____
_____
_____
_____
_____
_____
_____
_____
_____
_____
_____
_____

WHY ARE YOU WAITING TO EXHALE
When Everything that Has Breath Is Required to Praise the Lord?

Exercising Your Vocal Cords to Sing New Songs of Praise

What is the tune that you hear coming from the breath of the Lord? He will bless you to respond in that same tone. It is so sweet for the Lord to hear this as He listens to the songs of praises you are singing. The melody you return to Him brings gladness to His heart, which brings glory to the Lord. What are the new songs you will serenade Him with today?

_____
_____
_____
_____
_____
_____
_____
_____
_____
_____
_____
_____
_____
_____
_____
_____

Chapter 3

Praising God at All Times in All Things

Prince and Princess

Scripture: Psalm 146:1–2
"<u>Praise</u> the L<small>ORD</small>! Praise the L<small>ORD</small>, O my <u>soul</u>! I will praise the L<small>ORD</small> while I <u>live</u>; I will <u>sing praises</u> to my <u>God</u> while I have my being." (NASB)

WHY ARE YOU WAITING TO EXHALE
When Everything that Has Breath Is Required to Praise the Lord?

PRAISING GOD AT ALL TIMES IN ALL THINGS

Praising God for Who He Is

*"O L*ORD*, our Lord, how <u>majestic</u> is thy name in all the <u>earth</u>, who hast displayed thy <u>splendor</u> above the <u>heavens</u>!"—Psalm 8:1 (NASB)*

The breath of God is the most powerful thing in the universe. The same breath of God that can show up as a destructive wind that kills and clears the foundations of the earth, the same breath that can chill or burn, can give life or take it away. When God breathes into you, you come to life. Life ends if He withholds His breath from you. His breath is the strong source of our life. God used it to vitalize humanity and to awaken the human mind and intellect so we can recognize that praising God is the very center of our lives.

Our mere breath is a symbol of our weakness and frailty, but since we now have the power of the tongue to speak life or death, when we use it to praise God as it was designed to do, our breath has the power to accomplish much. We speak life with the tongue of praise or speak death and destruction to our spiritual enemy as we use the praises of the Lord to clear out the very foundations of hatred, anger, malice, envy, disputes, dissensions, idolatry, and jealousy. We use God's words of praise, which are loving, gentle, encouraging, and kind, as we speak to those Satan uses to come against us. By counterattacking in this way, we confuse our enemy and stop him from going for the kill. Our breath of praise is a powerful sign of life, because it originated with the Lord God when He said *"Let there be"*...and it was!

Praise God and Bless the Name of the Lord
"I will extol thee, my <u>God</u>, O <u>King</u>: and I will <u>bless</u> thy name forever and ever. Every day I will bless thee, and I will praise thy name <u>forever and ever.</u>"—Psalm 145:1–2 (NASB)

We receive victory as we praise, because we can use the same breath to call upon the name of the Lord to declare His goodness and greatness or to cry out to Him in our time of need or trouble. God blessed us to use this same breath to become fruitful, multiply, and take authority by speaking of good things that are pure, loving, and of good report. We do this best when we speak of His loving-kindness, His grace, and His mercy. We can use this breath to praise God at all times and in all things when we pray without ceasing to seek God's favor or give praises of thanksgiving.

Philippians 4:8 says, *"Finally, brothers and sisters, whatever is true, whatever is noble, whatever is right, whatever is pure, whatever is lovely, whatever is admirable—if anything is excellent or praiseworthy—think about such things."* The only

WHY ARE YOU WAITING TO EXHALE
When Everything that Has Breath Is Required to Praise the Lord?

thing we can constantly think about that fits this description perfectly is the Lord Himself. We fulfill this Scripture when we exhale pure, admirable, and lovely praises to the only One who is noble, rightfully excellent, and worthy of all praise. Our breath has been perfectly blown into us so we can give the Lord perfect praise as we express who He is in all of His perfection.

Continuing to Praise God at All Times
"I will <u>bless</u> the L<small>ORD</small> at <u>all</u> <u>times</u>; His <u>praise</u> shall <u>continually</u> be in my <u>mouth</u>. My <u>soul</u> shall make its <u>boast</u> in the L<small>ORD</small> the humble shall <u>hear</u> it and <u>rejoice</u>."—Psalm 34:1–2 (NASB)

If you are seeking God's continued presence, all you have to do is humbly praise God at all times. Boast in the Lord! Praise God while the sun is shining in your life and when the clouds are dark. Praise Him when the winds are strong and the storms are blowing heavy in your life, because even the storms are praising God as commanded. They assist you in your praise because they help to remind you of God's power and greatness, and they remind God of His goodness in creation when He used His own breath to breathe into you with gladness in His heart. Magnify the Lord with me for He created you from the foundation of the world to bless you by exalting you above all with praise, because He promised never to leave you nor forsake you, come rain or shine.

Continue to Praise God in All Things
"<u>Shout joyfully</u> to <u>God</u>, all the <u>earth</u>. <u>Sing</u> the glory of His name; make His <u>praise</u> <u>glorious</u>. <u>Say</u> to God, How <u>awesome</u> are thy works! Because of the greatness of thy power Thine enemies will give feigned obedience to Thee."—Psalm 66:1–3 (NASB)

When you praise God continuously, you seek His face and His presence continually, desiring to be with Him at all times. Constant praise gives you the opportunity to remember all of the wonderful deeds He has done for you and the awesome promises made concerning you because of His great power, for He is the Lord your God who keeps His word, and His word is true.

According to Psalm 105:4–5, when you continue to seek the Lord in your praise, you receive the strength of the Lord. God wants you to come into the knowledge of His greatness and His almighty power. When you praise God continuously, it also helps you to remember His marvelous wonders which He has done. It will remind you that you can't do anything without the Lord, yet you can do all things through Christ who strengthens you. Praise gives you the opportunity to call upon His name to do His will, because you have learned of His deeds among His people.

The Four Seasons of Praise
"And he will be like a tree firmly planted by streams of water, which yields its fruit in its <u>season</u>. And its leaf does not wither; and in whatever he <u>does</u>, he prospers. The wicked are not so, but they are like chaff which the wind drives away"—Psalm 1:3–4

WHY ARE YOU WAITING TO EXHALE
When Everything that Has Breath Is Required to Praise the Lord?

As the seasons change, so should our praises change. Praises that flow with the seasons allows us to become fruitful and prosper in due season. The seasons you will experience are designed to make you aware of the goodness and greatness of the Lord of your life. Each experience should be accompanied by praises based on your personal testimonies of what you've gone through so you can share with others as they go through their seasons of praise.

Your seasons will change, because they come at different times and for different reasons based on what is presently occurring in your life. God allows these sudden adversities in our lives to get our undivided attention because we tend to ignore Him while doing our own thing in life. No matter what season you're in, God wants you to learn how to sing new songs of praises to Him during and after these times of personal change.

Seasons are necessary for us to continue to praise Him; otherwise we would feel like we are going through life all alone. Different spiritual weather conditions will make us remember that God has already forecasted our future, and He is still in control of everything going on in our lives no matter what weathermen say when they try to predict your future and tell you what adjustments you need to make to cope with things they can't control themselves. These so-called professionals with their different degrees can't control the different degrees of temperature that affect the changes in their own lives, and yet they will try to tell you how to live your life based on spiritual weather conditions that have caused natural disasters for them because they failed to allow God to take control of their lives.

Your testimony matters deeply. Others need to know that you made it through these various weather conditions and lived to boast in what the Lord did during them when you praised God with new songs of seasonal praise. You are a newsperson forecasting good news, so share your testimony so that when it comes time for others to shout, they already know how and what to shout about! When they experience their seasons changing, they won't end up declaring areas of their life a total disaster, because they are prepared for the change based on your testimony of praises.

The four seasons of praise give us plenty of opportunity to sing new songs. Each one is different in nature and calls for different songs of praise.

§ DURING WINTER SEASON §

There are praises that reflect the spiritual winters we experience as cold and rainy seasons come. During these times, we will experience heavy snowstorms from the dark clouds forming over us, or heavy rain that threatens to drown us in the constant tears we shed. We will experience winds blowing against us to

WHY ARE YOU WAITING TO EXHALE
When Everything that Has Breath Is Required to Praise the Lord?

make us shiver in the trials and tribulations that come strongly against us. If we fail to put on enough of God's Word to cover us with a blanket of security to keep us warm inside, the winds could make us tired, weary, worn out, and even ready to give up. But praise God, our breath is strong and powerful enough to inhale His Word that will not return void!

The Word will supernaturally accomplish what God has said it will do. It will handle all these winter situations and circumstances when we continue to cry out to the Lord and speak out prayer and praise. His Word will superbly cover you so that you can wait on the Lord for warmer days.

This whole season is designed to remind us that our God is stronger than the winds and storms coming against us, greater than any hailstorm or blizzard we may face. He can speak to the winds and the waves to rebuke and bind them by speaking a word of peace to cover our lives. He can bring stillness in the storm long enough for us to get an understanding that we must keep praising Him. He can speak a word against those coming against us that will be so strong on our behalf it will stop the attack. Those attacking us will have to obey the power of His command. These winter conditions cause us to run for cover, and praise God, we have Someone powerful enough to run to for shelter, warmth, comfort, and strength.

This is why the Lord has also chosen to go through the storms with us as we take shelter and refuge within Him. He reminds us that greater is He within us than he and all that comes against us from the world. We may experience hell during this season, but we are strong little rocks built on the strong foundation of *the* Rock where we stand. We get to praise God for being the Rock of our salvation and our Cornerstone, always in our corner to protect and defend us. We are being built up with the strength to handle and resist those forces of evil that try to tear us down, and they will not prevail against us. Remember, this too shall pass because of the peace that surpasses all our understanding. Peace will comfort us and then go past us to handle the turbulence ahead. It will make the way straight for us to experience the peace that will keep us on the right path during this season.

We can praise God with wisdom and knowledge like Solomon, the wisest man on earth. He knew to praise God when he exhaled the Song of Solomon 2:11–12, which says, *"For lo, the winter is past, the rain is over and gone. The flowers appear on the earth; the time of singing has come, and the voice of the turtledove is heard in our land."*

God will dry all your tears so you won't wither up inside, and you will prosper and bloom here on earth to show the beauty of what you have become. The hardships of winter have caused you to blossom into a beautiful creature that was fearfully and wonderfully made in God's image, able to sing with a voice like the turtledove. Your song will encourage others for such a time as this. Your rainy season is over, and your winter season will soon be gone. You now have to get ready for the Spring.

§ *DURING SPRING SEASON* §

After the spiritual Winter season we come out of, we will experience times when our praises begin to spiritual spring up. Brighter days arrive as the Son comes out to shine in your life because of the hard times that took place during the Winter.

By spring you can show some new growth in your life. After being pruned, you can begin to show the fruit of your labor as a branch attached to the Tree of Life. You will produce more fruit during this season because the pruning allowed for healthier growth and your fruit has now multiplied in the areas that were pruned, showing off your maturity through stronger and healthier fruit.

Because of the Lord's pruning, you are able to grow into your full potential in that area of your life where God was working. You are able to give stronger and healthier praises to the Lord from this area. The fruit of your life now is sweeter and worth enjoying. Many will be able to hear those sweet praises and pick you out from among others who are not ready to be picked due to their bitterness or lack of growth. You will be full of sweet fruit, a gift of life ready for others as you become fruitful and multiplied in dominion spiritually. You will continue to labor in the love and the name of the Lord with praise and gift-giving, because it will be better for you to give than to receive. It is the Lord who has been working in you to create all of that sweetness that flows out of you to be a blessing to all.

Spring is a time for leaping and jumping for joy because of the fruit of the Spirit that has blossomed in you as you show an abundance of love, joy, peace, forbearance, kindness, goodness, faithfulness, gentleness, and self-control. This fruit is large and juicy because of your willingness to be fruitful in it. It has been produced in you by the Holy Spirit who comes from the Son, and His watering system comes from heaven like the spring rain mentioned in Hosea 6:3, which draws you closer to the Son.

Spiritual spring is a great time in our lives to be close to the Son. During this season we will be under pressure, and our fruit will be squeezed to show the seeds of faith that are yielding in us and to let us know what must be done for us to continue to grow by faith spiritually and manifest it physically. *"Let us press on to know the LORD,"* Hosea said. *"His going forth is as certain as the dawn; and He will come to us like the rain, like the spring rain watering the earth."*

WHY ARE YOU WAITING TO EXHALE
When Everything that Has Breath Is Required to Praise the Lord?

You can praise God that you get to reap this blessing after you have sown seeds of faith and invested them when you applied the Word of God to your life. Now others get to enjoy your maturity as your life productively multiplies, and you get to take your praise to higher heights! It is a higher praise to the Lord when you go with Him on the Great Commission into all the world, planting seeds of faith as you preach the gospel to every creature by ministering, witnessing, and evangelizing the discouraged and backslidden, whose fruit has fallen on unfertile ground. You have the privilege to assist the Lord as a disciple to seek and save the lost (Mark 16:14). It will be a higher praise, because you will be going in the name of the Lord with the Holy Spirit dwelling and growing within you a higher calling to cast out demons, to speak with new tongues, to take up serpents and not be hurt by them, to lay hands on the sick, and to accomplish greater works based on your faith in Christ. Higher praise will come forth because the Lord has done and is continuing to do a greater work within you (Mark 16:17–20) so you can yield greater praises as you produce greater fruit.

God wants us to recognize the truth of Psalm 85:9–13: *"Surely His salvation is near to those who fear Him, that glory may dwell in our land. Lovingkindness and truth have met together; righteousness and peace have kissed each other. Truth springs from the earth; and righteousness looks down from heaven.*

Indeed, the LORD *will give what is good; and our land will yield its produce. Righteousness will go before Him, and will make His footsteps into a way."* Your yielding to the Holy Spirit in this season is to guide you and grow you to bring you into all truth so you can spring with some pep in your step in the footsteps of Christ, who has already paved and walked this way of salvation. He knows what it takes to keep you safe and secure on this pathway. You will come directly into contact with His kisses of righteousness and peace, along with experiences of His lovingkindness and the goodness that He has already planted along the way for you to experience. You will pick up more opportunities to praise Him as you walk this path, because the plans of the Lord for your life are laid on this road in solid concrete. His plans for you are meant to last! They can't be washed away like sand, because they are structured to keep you walking by faith and not by sight. As long as you stay on this course, paved with the righteousness and cemented with the love and compassion of Jesus Christ, our Lord, you will experience on purpose all of God's plans for your life.

Springtime is a good time for higher praises to God as we joyously draw water from the springs of our salvation. In that day, you will remember what the prophet Isaiah said in Isaiah 12:3–4: that we are to exhale and *"Give thanks to the* LORD, *call on His name. Make known His deeds among the peoples; make them remember that His name is exalted. Praise the* LORD *in song, for*

WHY ARE YOU WAITING TO EXHALE
When Everything that Has Breath Is Required to Praise the Lord?

He has done excellent things; let this be known throughout the earth."

Isaiah knew based on what the Lord had impressed upon his heart that you and I were going to need this encouraging prophecy sooner or later in our future lives. The spring season of higher praises is our watering source, especially when we are thirsting for God's love, compassion, righteousness, and a better way of life. Springtime is for us when we need that kiss of peace from the Lord to comfort us along the way as we are cut off from those things or people that make us feel comfortable but will suck all the life out of us if they remain attached to us. Often, people or things want us to meet their needs instead of turning to the Lord and having Him supply what they need to spring forth in life as He expects them to do in His name.

If you are not careful during this season, you will find yourself in disobedience by always meeting their needs and not meeting the need the Lord has called you to in His will. If you don't stay focused on Christ, you will be left outside the will of God in this condition, leaving you dry and withered up, worn out, tired and weary from all elements of others' commands. This will cause you to compromise by trying to please them instead of them allowing you to be pleasing to the Lord so that His will and not their will can be done in your life.

When your priorities are misdirected in this way, you begin to look lifeless and thirsty, with an appearance like hard and dried-up fruit, because you lack the spring water from heaven that you were supposed to take in to refresh you during this season of change. This can cause you to wither up inside and draw you away from God. Others took advantage of your season of plenty, and now you can't praise God because you are withdrawn and dry from being so busy doing so much for so many that you failed to take care of yourself and spend more time with the Lord so you could continue in the strength of the Lord. You can be so busy that you can't give God your best praise or best service. A lack of the water from the Word during this time of change will leave you unrestored. However, praise God, for summertime is just around the corner!

We all seem to like summer. It gives us a chance to be refreshed, change clothes, change activities, and get out into the open to take in more of the Son, who shines bright in us to fill our lives with a brighter light and showcase all that is within us due to our period of restoration. But even in summertime the living may not be easy, because you will be exposed to all the elements of the world and the forces of evil coming against you. Take it from Matthew 24:32: *"Now learn the parable from the fig tree; when its branch has already become tender, and puts forth its leaves, you know that summer is near; even so you too, when you see all these things, recognize that He is near, right at the door."*

WHY ARE YOU WAITING TO EXHALE
When Everything that Has Breath Is Required to Praise the Lord?

§ *DURING SUMMER SEASON* §

By the time the spiritual Summer season rolls around, you will have gone through what it takes to weather the various storms in your life. You can take in and experience the summer breeze of the Lord's breath blowing within you, causing you to praise God. The Son feels so good in our lives during this season!

However, don't get too comfortable and forget to praise God for better days by laying around doing nothing, or by laying out in the open unprotected while in the Son. Even in summer, some days will be too hot for you to handle. Still, we know that there is nothing new under the sun, nothing that will take God by surprise. He has already provided us with a shade that can protect us from getting burned. Satan may start a fire to get you all heated up and burned out, but protection is here for you. The stormy and rainy seasons may be over right now, but this season can be very dry. If there is no water in sight, you may find yourself in an inner wilderness or desolated from being in a dry desert state of confusion.

You will need to put on the faith you have in Christ as your shield. Get under the Son so He can cover you and screen out all the rays of the heat coming against you from the gates of hell. God wants you to prevail and not get struck by your adversary's fiery darts so you can follow in the image of Christ as you walk in His footsteps in faith that are left in the sand during this time by staying on the path that was paved for you during your spiritual spring season.

The full armor of God is sunscreen that covers our entire body, and we need to put it on! We will be out in the open and the ground will seem shaky, but we will need to be able to do all to stand firm against all the evil schemes of the devil. This is the time to gird your waist with truth, put on the breastplate of righteousness, shod (bind) your feet with the preparation of the gospel of peace, and above all, take the shield of faith to cover you up, because it will allow you to extinguish all the flaming arrows coming from Satan, the evil one, and his heated weapons of mass destruction that will form against you. Take your helmet of salvation, along with the sword of the Spirit, which is the Word of God, while praying at all times in the Spirit. Be watchful to victory with all perseverance and supplication. This instruction for all the saints of God was exhaled to us in Ephesians 6:11–18 so that we may inhale its truths and exhale the praises of victory in advance. It is our privilege to give glory to the Son for shining bright in our lives and shielding us from all harm and danger, seen and unseen, for Satan is a defeated foe walking on shaky ground, who will burn in the end.

Armor is necessary because we are walking in the valley of the shadow of death, but we are instructed to fear no evil because

WHY ARE YOU WAITING TO EXHALE
When Everything that Has Breath Is Required to Praise the Lord?

God is with us as we shadow Him by continuing to walk in His footsteps by faith. When you follow His steps by imitating Christ, you will experience the authenticity of the beautiful shade of white clouds forming over you by day to keep you from feeling deserted or from drying up inside, and a glorious fire burning within you by night as you camp out with the Lord. The Lord wants to start a fire within you to be your guide by night and keep you warm during the midnight hour, even on your darkest days. He is the Faithful One whom we can always depend on due to the authenticity of His Word.

Therefore, little children, you don't have to be afraid of the dark! God is with us, and His rod and staff will comfort us during the cloudy days of this spiritual season. You must allow the Son to shine brightly within you so this guiding light can start a fire inside your heart. You must keep shining bright to show your light to others in this world of darkness. This is the only way to let your little light shine for all the world to see, so don't hide your light by drawing up inside. The world needs to be drawn to the Light by your praise and thanksgiving due to the Light shining in your life.

Seasons come and seasons go, and so will our praises to the Lord—they come in at the right time and go out at the right time as we use the breath within us to express the goodness of the Lord. Scripture tells us in Genesis 8:22 that *"While the earth remains, seedtime and harvest, and cold and heat, and summer and winter, and day and night shall not cease."* We can expect these seasons and the weather conditions that accompany them to come and go continuously as they were designed to do so that we may give God glory in due season. We need to be prepared to plant seeds of faith at the right time and in the right place, so they can be watered and give opportunity for God to give the increase. Then we can receive a harvest that crops up and flourishes within us as it nourishes all those who feed off our lives when we are being fruitful during this season with praise.

When you plant your seed of praise, you can expect that praise to come back to bring you a harvest full of blessings. You can gather these blessings up and share them with others while walking on the right path. This route has been paved with God's love and compassion. There are many who may need your support of love and compassion in their off-season while they wait for their crops, planted in fertile ground, to grow into blessings.

The seeds of praise will be fruitful to produce and multiply much more praise. You can continue to produce more praises to God, and He will continue to give you a multitude of reasons to praise Him even more! Christ Jesus will become your Water of Life, watering every seed of faith that you plant in Him. This season is important because you will need to be ready for the next season of change. If you made it through the Summer, praise God!

WHY ARE YOU WAITING TO EXHALE
When Everything that Has Breath Is Required to Praise the Lord?

Get ready, for the Fall is coming. The blessings you experience now were designed and watered by the Lord to be fruitful and to produce the fruit of their kind within you. This is the reason for the season! We were commanded to be fruitful, multiply, and take dominion in the things that God gave us to labor over in this land of promise, so we will not fall. As we harvest blessings and share them, we can do our part to fill the earth with His praises.

§ *DURING FALL SEASON* §

In the spiritual Fall season, we need to continue to build a strong and solid foundation based on the Word of God. If you are not steadfast in your belief and trust in the Lord with all your heart, you can easily fall into sinful situations that will cause you to become like the leaves on a tree in autumn: dying and disconnected from the source of life. Like those leaves that have turned and fallen from their only connection to life, in our hearts, we too can turn from God. Separation from the Lord during this season leaves us looking lifeless due to sin. During this spiritual season of change where leaves are turning and appear different, we have to be very careful not to turn away from God. We must be careful not to turn and appear different by staying closely connected, because if we fall into sin, we too can end up far away from the life God had planned, planted, and prepared that was rooted in us to continue to stay connected and be lifted up in Him.

If your foundation is weak in various areas of your life, you need to lean more strongly on the Lord to give you the life support you need. Brace yourself and let the Lord continue to work on all your weaknesses—to strengthen anything that, left weak, would cause your heart to break and your countenance to fall.

You can become stronger in the Lord by inhaling every instruction from the Word of God. Stay attached to the structure of God that's being built in your life by reading, remembering, and ready to proclaim the Word. We are commanded to stay connected to Him in our hearts and minds, because He is doing a great work in us to keep us grounded in His Word so that we can't be moved by any problem, temptation, or sinful situation that would cause our temple to spiritually turn away, fall down, broken and die.

Stop focusing on all that is going on around you. Stop listening to those who would tear down your walls of faith, because they will weaken your joints during the fall. Don't put your faith in man, but abide in God to remain standing strong. Psalm 125:1–2 has been exhaled to let us know that *"Those who trust in the* LORD *are as Mount Zion, which cannot be moved, but abides forever. As the mountains surround Jerusalem, so the* LORD *surrounds His people from this time forth and forever."*

The fall represents things dying in our lives, but as long as

WHY ARE YOU WAITING TO EXHALE
When Everything that Has Breath Is Required to Praise the Lord?

you are strongly rooted in the Word of God, you can strongly count on Him. You will receive the promise if you believe Him when He says that He will never leave you nor forsake you, because His Word is true, and that truth will set you free from the deadly weather conditions during this season. Believe that God never changes, because He is not a man that He should lie and have to repent. Believing this, you can receive what you believe and get the strength you need during this season of change. You won't fall for anything or sin against God. You won't spiritually die inside, because you know God is just working on you and that you can get through the pruning stage. God is cutting off that which will weaken you if you stay attached to it. Separation from God due to deadly and sinful situations that will ultimately destroy your life and your relationship with the Lord God is a terrible thing. God is pruning these things away from you so that you can remain strong in Him during the fall.

These seasonal praises should remind you of the covenant between you and God, made when you accepted Christ as your personal Lord and Savior. This covenant was from the beginning. It started with Abraham; was given as an oath to Isaac; and was confirmed through Jacob. It was everlasting to Joseph/Israel, and it has been extended to you through all generations. It is your task in this covenant to spread the seeds of blessing and praise throughout the land of promise. The promise will be fulfilled through you and your offspring as you sojourn in this world, because it involves your redemption from beginning to end. Therefore, during every spiritual season, remember to . . .

PERSONALLY PRAISE GOD WITH PRAISES THAT GO WITH EVERY SEASON TO BE EXHALED FROM EVERY CLIMATE CHANGE WITHIN YOU

Keep Breathing During Your Spiritual Winter Seasons of Change to Give God Praise

What have you learned about the spiritual winter season that will cause you to praise God during the winter and rainy storms in your life? What have you learned that will cause you to exhale praises to God and to share with others how you weathered the storms of life to praise the Lord with new songs?

_____
_____
_____
_____
_____
_____
_____
_____

WHY ARE YOU WAITING TO EXHALE
When Everything that Has Breath Is Required to Praise the Lord?

Keep Breathing During Your Spiritual Spring Seasons of Change to Give God Praise

What have you learned about the spiritual spring season? What has God pruned from your life to cause you to exhale praises to Him as you experience new growth of maturity? What fruit do you see growing that causes you to spring up and multiply your praises to the Lord with a dominion of new songs?

_____
_____
_____
_____
_____
_____
_____
_____
_____
_____
_____
_____
_____
_____
_____
_____
_____
_____
_____
_____

Keep Breathing During Your Spiritual Summer Seasons of Change to Give God Praise

What have you learned about the spiritual summer season? What must you do while out in the open to protect yourself from the heat that will burn you? You can praise God during summer weather conditions that require Son-screen to be put on. How can you follow the instructions as to how to apply this to your life that will cause you to exhale praises to the Lord with new songs?

_____
_____
_____
_____
_____
_____
_____
_____
_____
_____
_____
_____
_____
_____
_____
_____
_____
_____
_____

WHY ARE YOU WAITING TO EXHALE
When Everything that Has Breath Is Required to Praise the Lord?

Keep Breathing During Your Spiritual Fall Seasons of Change to Give God Praise

What have you learned about the spiritual fall season that will keep you from turning from God and leave you falling into sinful situations? God exhaled promises and teachings in His Word that will keep you alive and breathing as you inhale them, because you are still connected during your weakest points in your life, and now you can exhale praises to the Lord with different new songs. What are these promises and teachings in your life?

_____
_____
_____
_____
_____
_____
_____
_____
_____
_____
_____
_____
_____
_____
_____
_____
_____
_____
_____

Chapter 4

Sing God a New Song of Praise Every Day

Prince and Princess

Scripture: Psalm 96:1–2
"<u>Sing</u> to the L<small>ORD</small> a new song; sing to the L<small>ORD</small>, all the <u>earth</u>. Sing to the L<small>ORD</small>, <u>bless</u> His name; proclaim good tidings of His salvation from day to day." (NASB)

WHY ARE YOU WAITING TO EXHALE
When Everything that Has Breath Is Required to Praise the Lord?

SING GOD A NEW SONG OF PRAISE EVERY DAY

The Sweet Smell of One Desiring to Properly Breathe with Praise

"Delight yourself in the LORD; and He will give you the <u>desires</u> of your <u>heart</u>. <u>Commit</u> your <u>way</u> to the LORD, trust also in Him, and He will do it."—Psalm 37:4–5 (NASB)

𝓐 sweet aroma comes from the praises of one who delights in the Lord. This means having a desire in your heart for God, a desire to do His will and trust in Him with all your heart. When you desire God, then God will give you Himself and all that is within His will for you to experience and know. You will know for yourself who He is, because you trust Him to do this.

When you exhale praises of delight, it is one of the sweetest things you can do. It is your evidence, both seen and heard, of that which you have assured in your heart for the Lord. It is the substance of your faith that you hope will be pleasing to Him because you want Him to fill your heart with His precious love and will for your life.

God doesn't need any other reason to bless you! When you commit to Him in all of your ways, committing to obey Him just because it is His will, it is a sign of your trust in Him and your desire to love Him with all your heart, mind, body, soul and strength.

When you desire the Lord, you will also receive the precious promise that you will live with Him for all eternity, and with that comes all the precious promises of God for those who partake of the Lord's divine nature. He will honor your desire for Him because it is based on your trust in the promise of His Word. This promise is found in the plan of your salvation from the foundation of the world, and He has kept that promise by giving Himself for you through His Only Begotten Son. This was God's will to save you, and that's exactly what He did so that you could trust Him when He asked you to believe and receive the gift of life from the only Giver of life. Having received this life, now it's time to praise Him with it.

Finding reasons to praise God every day shows your delight in the Lord and your desire to be in His presence daily. Exodus 15:2 says it best for us to express: *"I will praise Him."* The praise should be personal and come from your very lips according to Psalm 63:3. The book of Psalms is full of new songs of praise, and God expects us to use them daily as we serenade Him for who He is, for what He did, and for what He means to us as He reveals Himself to us. The praises come from the assembly of His faithful people, who faithfully seek Him daily due to His faithfulness.

WHY ARE YOU WAITING TO EXHALE
When Everything that Has Breath Is Required to Praise the Lord?

Those who desire Him know that they can always put their trust in the promises found in His Word.

God looks forward to hearing from us daily. He is concerned about the daily affairs of the lives He gave us, and He looks forward to expressing His love and compassion for us by giving us our daily bread, filled with His supply of life to strengthen us daily as we exhale praises to Him to get us through the day. He has a great desire for us to know Him as the Great I Am by giving us new songs of praise. He will be everything we need Him to be every day as we go through life with Him.

Singing Praises Is for Your Good
"<u>Praise</u> the L<small>ORD</small>! For it is <u>good</u> to <u>sing</u> <u>praises</u> to our God; for it is pleasant and <u>praise</u> is <u>becoming</u>."— Psalm 147:1 (NASB)

In Psalm 147 you can see that your praises to our Lord are for your good, because they are pleasant and becoming to the Lord. They give Him glory, because they tell of the Lord's ability to do what seems impossible for us. He can heal the brokenhearted and bind up their wounds. These praises are due to the Lord, because they tell of His greatness, His abundant strength, His understanding that is infinite, and His support for the afflicted as He mends those whose hearts are broken and brings down the wicked to the ground.

We praise God with our thanksgiving when we sing praises to the Lord because He is the One who covers the heavens with clouds and provides rain for the earth, who makes grass to grow on the mountains, who gives food to the beasts of the field and to the young ravens who cry out. He is the God whose Word can send forth His commands to the earth. His Word runs swiftly to fulfill all of His ordinances to prosper us here on earth and to make peace in our borders. The Lord shows favor to those who praise Him while they wait for His loving-kindness to satisfy them. He is their Shepherd, and they shall not want (Psalm 23:1).

We find in 1 Chronicles 16:25 a confirmation of all of this. This psalm of thanksgiving, starting in verse 8, expresses that God is great and greatly to be praised. It begins with giving thanks to the Lord by calling upon His name and making all of His deeds known by first singing praises to Him and then speaking of all His wonders in the presence of others. We become spiritually fruitful when we speak to others with love, joy, peace, patience, kindness, goodness, faithfulness, gentleness, and self-control, expressing our faithfulness to the Lord, which is a testimony of our praise. In edifying others with your mouth and serving them like Christ came to do, you are reflecting the same love and compassion God has for the world to experience.

God has given us the privilege to call upon His name, and He tells us to boast in the Lord God so that we can multiply the

WHY ARE YOU WAITING TO EXHALE
When Everything that Has Breath Is Required to Praise the Lord?

fruitfulness of our praises as He draws all men unto Himself. The glory in exhaling praises in this way is in taking dominion to glorify His holy name. When you seek the Lord to praise Him as He reveals Himself to you, the benefit for you will be to receive gladness in your heart because you are coming into the knowledge of who God is. You will realize the strength of the Lord that is in you when you show reverence to Lord God and see others drawn to Him for salvation.

God's breath was full of new praises from the beginning. His Word, who is the Lord, can also exhale into you the newest of life. I personally experienced this several years ago when I was spending fifteen to thirty minutes with God every day in my morning devotions and then spending anywhere from two to four hours a day in the evening studying God's Word. One morning during my devotional I was reading Psalm 96:1, which exhaled the same breath of God that was repeated in Psalm 98:1, which expresses how important it is that we sing to the Lord a new song of praise because of the marvelous things He has done with His right hand and His holy arm to save us.

On that morning while I read about singing to the Lord a new song, God took the opportunity to tell me that my praises were stale. When I asked Him why He felt this way, He spoke to my heart and said that I spent all this time with Him every day, and yet

I praised Him as if I really didn't know Him. When I examined my daily praises, I found out that I was praising Him with the same three or four praises every day.

As I continued my conversation with God while meditating on what He said, I asked Him what He wanted me to sing. He said to use the words of the songs that are written in His Word because they beautifully express who He is. I was to go get a pen to write down my praises as He revealed Himself to me.

When I went to get some paper, I thought this was going to be a Moses moment where I needed to get a tablet to write down a command from God. Instead, God spoke to my heart that when He revealed Himself in my Bible, I was to write down my praises right then and there at the same place He revealed Himself to me. Psalm 45:1–2 confirmed that *"My tongue is the pen of a ready writer . . . grace is poured upon thy lips."* When I came to that place in my Bible again, I would already know what to sing. I would write down my new song while in His presence, and that way I would be reminded of who He is.

Journaling in this way is powerful. God wants us to see it in our own writing so we don't lose track of what the Lord has revealed to us about Himself. I was also being trained to know what to say whenever I came across this same situation in my life, because I would be reminded that God is with me and I would already know how to praise Him in my heart while in His

WHY ARE YOU WAITING TO EXHALE
When Everything that Has Breath Is Required to Praise the Lord?

presence. These praises were now perfectly prepared by God to be exhaled because they come from a pure heart to declare who He is to me.

A Celebration with Praise Songs

"My <u>heart</u> overflows with a <u>good</u> <u>theme</u>; I <u>address</u> my verses to the <u>King</u>; my tongue is the pen of a ready <u>writer</u>."—Psalm 45:1 (NASB)

After three years of writing down my praises to God in my Bible as He revealed Himself, I could no longer read this Bible because of all of the praises that had come from my lips! When I got up one morning, instead of praising God, I got up to complain. I told the Lord that I'd spent sixty-five dollars for this Bible, and now I could no longer read His Word for all of these . . . then I stopped. I had just learned with great wisdom from God that God paid a much greater price so that I could praise Him continually, even through my difficulties, and that His Word He exhaled was full of praises for me to experience. That's when He told me that He had been exhaling praises into me during my reading and studying as He revealed Himself to me, and now that I was trained in the way that I should go, He was just waiting for me to exhale.

Singing the psalms as praise songs deepens your intimacy with the Lord and heightens your devotion to Him. It's an inspirational celebration of praise that will cause you to eagerly seek Him in all of His ways to draw closer to Him, and it will teach you how to worship and honor God properly as you praise Him. So you learned to . . .

Practice Singing New Songs as You Exhale with Praise

What new songs have you learned that can give the Lord pleasure in knowing that your heart is full of praise for Him? Write down the praises you can exhale every day to fill His heart as you celebrate the newness of your life with wisdom and thanksgiving.

_____
_____
_____
_____
_____
_____
_____
_____
_____
_____
_____
_____
_____
_____
_____
_____

WHY ARE YOU WAITING TO EXHALE
When Everything that Has Breath Is Required to Praise the Lord?

Chapter 5

Wisdom Is Found in the Praises of His People

Prince and Princess

Scripture: Psalm 105:1–2
"Oh <u>give thanks</u> to the L<small>ORD</small>, <u>call</u> upon His name; <u>make known</u> His deeds among the <u>peoples</u>. <u>Sing</u> to Him, <u>sing praises</u> to Him; <u>speak</u> of all His <u>wonders</u>." (NASB)

WHY ARE YOU WAITING TO EXHALE
When Everything that Has Breath Is Required to Praise the Lord?

WISDOM IS FOUND IN THE PRAISES OF

HIS PEOPLE

The Excellency of Brotherly Unity in Praise
"Behold, how <u>good</u> and how pleasant it is for brothers to dwell together in unity! It is like the <u>precious</u> oil upon the head, coming down upon the <u>beard</u>."—Psalm 133:1 (NASB)

When we speak to one another, we are to do so with wisdom, speaking praises of psalms, hymns, and songs from the Spirit. This will cause us to sing and make beautiful music from our hearts as unto the Lord according to Ephesians 5:19. As Christians, our conduct should be according to 1 Thessalonians 5:16: we are to rejoice always, pray without ceasing, and in everything give thanks, for this is God's will for us in Christ Jesus. A lifestyle of constant praise keeps us from quenching the Holy Spirit who dwells within us. We will be empowered to continue to praise God, because Scripture says in verses 20 and 21 that we do this by *"always giving thanks for all things in the name of our Lord Jesus Christ to God, even the Father; and be subject to one another in the fear of Christ."*

We must guard our hearts and minds in order to guard our tongues and our ways. There is life and death in the tongue. When we fail to use the breath of life to speak good and not evil, we fall prey to the vanity of life. Psalm 39 exhales truth to assist us with this. *"I said, 'I will <u>guard</u> my <u>ways</u>, that I may not sin with my tongue; I will <u>guard</u> my <u>mouth</u> as with a muzzle, while the <u>wicked</u> are in my presence.'"* We can instruct ourselves to consult with the Lord and continue to say, *"Then I <u>spoke</u> with my tongue: 'LORD, make me to know my end, and what is the extent of my <u>days</u>, let me know how transient I am. Behold, thou hast made my days as handbreadths, and my <u>lifetime</u> as nothing in thy sight. Surely every <u>man</u> at his <u>best</u> is a mere breath. Selah!" (NASB)*

When you are caught up in the vanity of life, it is a sign that the lust of the flesh, the lust of the eye, and the pride of life are ruling in you. You have a desire to be praised by others instead of joining others to praise the Lord for all He has done that you could not have done without Him! When you seek the praises of others as opposed to giving God all the praises, you are not breathing properly. Instead of desire and delight, you are now giving God a sign that you are vain as you withhold your breath of praise, waiting to exhale because you want someone to lift *you* up in praise. Those who think more highly of themselves than they ought to think will not be lifted up in praise by the Lord.

WHY ARE YOU WAITING TO EXHALE
When Everything that Has Breath Is Required to Praise the Lord?

The Vain Have Bad Breath

"O <u>sons</u> of <u>men</u>, how long will my <u>honor</u> become a reproach? How long will you <u>love</u> what is worthless and aim at <u>deception</u>? But know that the LORD has <u>set apart</u> the <u>godly</u> man for Himself; the LORD hears when I call to Him."—Psalm 4:2 (NASB)

The vain have bad breath because they refuse to give God praise for anything, either because they don't know who God is—in which case they end up believing and praising themselves rather than believing in the Lord—or simply because they are holding their breath and refusing to exhale praises to the Lord. You often hear them say that they are self-made and have gained everything they think they own on their own.

The vanity of life will cause you to walk around thinking you are higher than you ought to think. You will make an uproar for nothing because you are full of yourself—but you are nothing but dust. You rejoice in your own foolishness and do not realize that you are perishing because of a lack of knowledge—not of good and evil, but of who Christ is, of who you are supposed to be in Christ, and of what you were designed to do for Christ. The vanity of life makes us strangers with God, and our gaze is not on the tree of life but on the tree of the knowledge of good and evil. We think that we can physically reach for something spiritual in nature and become spiritually satisfied without God. We have a desire to taste that which is pleasing in our sight without tasting to see that the Lord is good.

When you go after your own desires, it leaves a bad taste in your mouth! It will cause bad breath due to the evil that is attached to that which looks good but is bad for you. Psalm 2:1 asks, *"Why do the nations conspire and the peoples plot in vain?"* Instead of praising God for allowing you to experience whatever you are going through, you end up with a bad taste in your mouth because you want to blame God for the choices you have made in vain, choices based on your desires and not His. When that turns out to be bad for you, you will not give God praise. However, God will sustain His servants to wait patiently for Him according to Psalm 40, because He has inclined His ear to hear their cry and respond by bringing them out of the pit of destruction, satisfying them with a taste of the goodness that He has placed on the tree of life for them to keep them both spiritually and physically alive as they continue to focus on the Lord based on their desire to please Him and not themselves.

The Lord lets us all know in Psalm 127:2 that *"In vain you rise early and stay up late, toiling for food to eat—for he grants sleep to those he loves."* This lifestyle happens when we rush about, heaping up wealth without knowing whose it will finally be. The Lord ends the days of such people in futility and their years in terror according to Psalm 78:33. However, praises go to the Lord,

WHY ARE YOU WAITING TO EXHALE
When Everything that Has Breath Is Required to Praise the Lord?

because He has ordered His children's steps and made them firm to follow Him in all His ways and commandments.

Psalm 119:37 gives an illustration of what it means to go after worthless things based on your own desires. It commands you to ask the Lord to *"Turn my eyes away from worthless things; preserve my life according to your word."* God's desire is to make known to you the path of life. He will fill you with joy in His presence with eternal pleasures that are located at His right hand. We can truly serve the Lord with gladness because we know who He is and who we are in Christ as we serve Him. He is the *Way*, the *Truth*, and the *Life* (John 14:6)!

In the New Testament Peter exhaled praises to God for all to hear. Second Peter 1:2 says, *"Grace and peace in this life be multiplied to you in the knowledge of God and of Jesus our Lord; seeing that His divine power has granted to us everything pertaining to life and godliness, through the true knowledge of Him who called us by His own glory and excellence."* In this new covenant between you and God, you can praise the Lord because His divine power has given you everything you need to be who He has called you to be in Him.

The Lord has placed everything we need to succeed in us. He has given us *Himself,* and He is waiting for us to exhale praises as we place our life in Him and yield to that which pertains to life and godliness. The divine nature was put into us through the knowledge of the Lord, who is the Word of God, because He has called us by His glory to live the kind of life He has ordained. He gave us His Spirit and the knowledge of His Word with the capacity to understand it, so that it will be union in the communion with God. When we keep reading His Word over and over again until we have exhausted it, we come to an understanding of His Word with wisdom to fully exhale praises to His name.

Praises Come from the Servants of the Lord

"<u>Praise</u> the Lord! Praise the name of the Lord; praise Him, O <u>servants</u> of the Lord, you who stand in the <u>house</u> of the LORD, in the courts of the house of our <u>God</u>! Praise the Lord, for the Lord is <u>good</u>; <u>sing praises</u> to His name for it is lovely."—Psalm 135:1–3 (NASB)

Holy and awesome is the name of the Lord. The true knowledge of this comes from having the fear of the Lord, and a good understanding comes to all those who serve the Lord in love and apply God's Word to do His commandments. Psalm 100:2 reminds us of this as it exhorts us that we are to serve the Lord with gladness and come before Him with joyful singing. We can only do this because we know that the Lord Himself is God and that it is He who has made us and not we ourselves. It is He who has saved us and made us into His image and likeness, and He wants us to imitate Him, because He came to earth not to be served but to serve.

WHY ARE YOU WAITING TO EXHALE
When Everything that Has Breath Is Required to Praise the Lord?

It is wise to give praise and serve the God of our salvation, because it is He who delivered us from all unrighteousness. Psalm 30 tells us that the Lord has not let our enemies rejoice over us. We can cry to Him for help, and He will not only hear us but heal us. He has brought up our souls from Sheol and kept us alive in Him. We can rest in our salvation and sing praises to the Lord because He considers us His godly ones, and we will not be going down to the pit of hell. We can trust this word with thanksgiving, because the Lord's favor is for a lifetime! Even though weeping may endure for a night, a shout of joy will come in the morning. We can prosper with this word, because we can never be moved or taken out of the hands of our Lord and Savior Jesus Christ.

We can continue to speak with this wisdom because God did not give us a spirit of fear, but of love, power, and a sound (disciplined) mind. We all know that the beginning of wisdom is the fear of the Lord. So my brothers and sisters in the Lord, praise God for wisdom and . . .

Don't stop spiritually breathing to exhale praises to the LORD GOD, because every second that God exhales the breath of life full of praises into you so that you may experience His goodness, remember that He is waiting for you to exhale PRAISES as a sign of life! He is waiting to experience personally the breath coming from your praises. May God continue to exhale His

breath into you to extend your life so you can continue to **BREATHE AND EXHALE PRAISES TO THE LORD GOD . . .** *HALLELUJAH and AMEN!*

Expressing Wisdom as You Exhale Sweet Songs of Praise

As a believer and a servant in the body of Christ, what wisdom have you inhaled from the Lord that you can now share with others as you boast in Him to assist in filling the earth with the praises of the Lord through your testimonies of wisdom and thanksgiving?

_____
_____
_____
_____
_____
_____
_____
_____
_____
_____
_____
_____
_____
_____

WHY ARE YOU WAITING TO EXHALE
When Everything that Has Breath Is Required to Praise the Lord?

Showing Others How to Breath as You Exhale Sweet Songs of Praise

To assist those who are waiting to exhale, write down your testimony of praise and practice your breathing techniques by exercising your vocal cords to prepare yourself to exhale praises about the Lord. Practice sharing what you have learned from the Lord and from His Word to express what He has done in your life to keep you alive and well in Him. The Lord will exhale the final praise, *"WELL DONE MY GOOD AND FAITHFUL SERVANT!"*

Confirmation from Matthew 25:21 exhaled *"His Lord said unto him, Well done, thou good and faithful servant: thou hast been faithful over a few things, I will make thee ruler over many things: enter thou into the joy of thy Lord." (KJV)*

_____
_____
_____
_____
_____
_____
_____
_____
_____
_____
_____
_____
_____
_____

Chapter 6

The Sinner's Prayer of Praise

Prince and Princess

Scripture: Psalm 107:1–3
"Oh <u>give thanks</u> to the L<small>ORD</small>, for He is <u>good</u>; for His <u>lovingkindness</u> is <u>everlasting</u>. Let the <u>redeemed</u> of the L<small>ORD</small> <u>say</u> so, whom He has redeemed from the <u>hand</u> of the adversary, and <u>gathered</u> from the <u>lands</u>, from the east and from the west, from the north and from the south."
(NASB)

WHY ARE YOU WAITING TO EXHALE
When Everything that Has Breath Is Required to Praise the Lord?

THE SINNER'S PRAYER OF PRAISE

The Lord Exalts the Humble Who Bow Down with Praise

"<u>Be gracious</u> to me, O <u>God</u>, according to thy lovingkindness; according to the greatness of thy <u>compassion</u> <u>blot</u> <u>out</u> my transgressions. Wash me thoroughly from my iniquity, and cleanse me from my sin. For I know my <u>transgressions</u>. <u>Wash</u> me thoroughly from my iniquity, and <u>cleanse</u> me from my <u>sin</u>. For I know my <u>transgressions</u>, and my sin is <u>ever</u> before me. Against thee, thee only, I have <u>sinned</u>, and <u>done</u> what is <u>evil</u> in thou sight, so that thou art <u>justified</u> when thou dost <u>speak</u>, and blameless when thou dost <u>judge</u>."—Psalm 51:1–4 (NASB)

𝒜𝓁𝓁 have sinned and fallen short of the glory of God. According to Psalm 51:5, *"I was brought forth in iniquity, and in sin my mother conceived me."* Therefore, in order for God to receive the praise of His glory, He had to prepare from the foundation of the world a way for Him to satisfy His desire of finding the truth in the innermost part of every human being, of making you know the wisdom of God, of purifying you and making you clean by washing you whiter than snow and giving you a new heart, a disciplined mind, and a right spirit within. This is what we call "salvation." The Lord wants you to hear the joy and gladness of His heart. He wants to cause the bones that were broken in you to rejoice, and in turn, He wants to hide Himself from your sins by blotting out all of your iniquities. He wants to create in you a clean heart and renew a steadfast spirit within you so He doesn't have to cast you away from His presence.

God did all this by giving you His Best, His Only Begotten Son, so that whosoever believes in His Son will receive eternal life to spend eternity with Him. That new life is the new spiritual creature, who will then be able to receive the Holy Spirit, who is the mind of Christ, to live within. When you have been made new and received the Holy Spirit, God can lead you into all truth according to His Word and restore the joy of His salvation by sustaining you with a willing spirit so that you may have delight in your heart for God and a desire to please God in this life. This Word of salvation came from the breath of the Lord. Jesus is the Word inhaled in you so you will humble yourself and bow down with praise for what the Lord has done to save you from damnation (John 3:16).

In God's Word you will find all the reasons in the world to praise Him. He desires to exhale this breath of salvation to all mankind so that we may all experience His mercy and His grace. Even the sinner has reason to praise the Lord. God has a joy to give us that no man can give and no man can take away, because it is found in the gift of life from the Giver of life. Because of His love and compassion for us, He wants us to be with Him for all eternity. His love and compassion will last a lifetime and beyond, because this love and compassion have produced His mercy and grace to give us the opportunity to give a praise report for what the Lord has done for us.

Mercy and Grace Produce Praise

"But thou, O LORD, art a <u>God</u> merciful and <u>gracious</u>, slow to anger and abundant in lovingkindness and truth."—Psalm 86:15 (NASB)

You will receive the tongue of joyfully singing the praises of God's righteousness by opening your lips and declaring with your own mouth His praises as you were originally designed to do. When you begin to express praises because of the mercy and grace of the Lord God, you are fulfilling your created purpose. It will not only set you free from sin's consequences, but from the power of it. That we might live exceeding above contempt, anger, fear, lust, covetousness, and dishonesty. This will surpass righteousness because it is the way to the kingdom of God.

You see, God is not pleased with burnt offerings, but with the sacrifices of a broken spirit and a broken and contrite heart. The Lord wants to be merciful and gracious to you. His Word reveals His heart for the sinner. God sees no profit in your blood if you go down to the pit, because the dust does not praise the Lord or declare His faithfulness. He wants you to know that He is gracious to those who cry out to Him to be their Helper. Psalm 30 is all about being thankful for being delivered from death. It is a prayer of help like the one found in Psalm 123:3: *"Be gracious to us, O LORD, be gracious to us; for we are greatly filled with contempt."* David exhaled these words because he had witnessed the Lord's grace, and he expressed this testimony to let you know that the Lord can change your mourning into dancing with gladness of heart. Your soul can sing praises to God forever and not wait to exhale praises by being silent.

You can graciously praise the Lord today, because you can receive new mercies every day. He has pardoned you from all of your iniquities and healed you from all of your diseases according to Psalm 103. He did this to redeem your life from the pit of hell, and He crowns you with loving-kindness and compassion because He wants to satisfy you with years of good things from Him. You can taste and see for yourself that the Lord is good, because you have been restored back to your original position when He first crowned you as head of His creation.

I shared this message with a group one morning, and an interesting comment came from my sister-in-love. She said that God had revealed to her during the message that even sinners know they are supposed to praise the Lord, because they too have His breath in them! She pointed out that we often hear and see

WHY ARE YOU WAITING TO EXHALE
When Everything that Has Breath Is Required to Praise the Lord?

sinners on award shows giving God praise for what they have accomplished in the world. We might consider what they have done in this world to be sinful and it to be an insult or blasphemy toward the Lord to mention God's name in vain by giving Him credit for what they have done, yet they know to praise God in spite of their sinful ways.

My sister-in-love repented for judging those who boast in the Lord by giving praises to God even when they do not know Him, because she realized that we should do the same! Even those who don't know God know they are required to exhale praises for who He is, even though they have not changed the way they live their dusty and raggedy lives (even though they think they have been turned from rags to riches). God said you can gain the whole world and still lose your soul; He has given everyone an equal opportunity to change their life by changing their thinking as to who He is and what He has done. God doesn't judge our outer appearance; it is the heart of man that He sees and is looking to change.

We often judge people from the outside, but we have no idea what's going on in the inside of someone's heart who praises the Lord even when their life tells a different story than ours. We must remember that God said that we were once lost sinners, and He found us. Like Christ we can hate the sin, but not the sinner whom He loves. As long as they have breath and are still alive to praise the Lord, God can still save them. Praise God!

Even the breath of a sinner in need of salvation is very significant, because in his present condition, he can cry out to the Lord for salvation. Sinners recognize the need to praise God with the breath of a sinner's praise and pray a prayer of repentance when they know that the Lord died and rose again with all power to raise them up from their deadly situation. They too have a desire to praise God for all eternity as they were designed to do from the beginning because of the breath of life that has been exhaled into them to live for Christ.

The Prayer of Praise from the Sinner's Breath

"__Be gracious__ to me, O LORD, for I am pining away; heal me, O LORD, for my __bones__ are __dismayed__. And my __soul__ is greatly dismayed; but thou, O LORD—how long? __Return__ O LORD, __rescue__ my soul; __save__ me because of thy lovingkindness. For there is no __mention__ of thee in __death__; in __Sheol__ who will give thee thanks?"— Psalm 6:2–5 (NASB)

This sinner's prayer is a prayer for mercy in your time of trouble because you know that you need a Savior and you can't save yourself. You have to put your faith in Christ, believing that if you pray for salvation, He will answer this prayer because His desire is that none should perish and be eternally separated from Him. You have to believe the love that He has in His heart for you.

WHY ARE YOU WAITING TO EXHALE
When Everything that Has Breath Is Required to Praise the Lord?

God wants you to come into the knowledge of Christ and what He has done to save you from eternal damnation, which is an eternal separation from Him.

Before you take your last breath; make sure you have given God your breath of praise for forgiving you of your sin and allowing you to praise Him for all eternity. Ask Him to show you His loving-kindness by being gracious to you, rescuing your soul from death so you won't have to experience the pit of hell. Ask Him to come into your life to exhale into you His breath, so that you may inhale it and be made spiritually alive to praise Him forever.

Nothing Dead in Sheol Can Exhale God's Praises of Thanksgiving

"For Sheol cannot <u>thank</u> thee, <u>Death</u> cannot <u>praise</u> thee; those who go down to the <u>pit</u> cannot hope for thy faithfulness. It is the living who give thanks to thee, as I do today; a father <u>tells</u> his <u>sons</u> about thy faithfulness.."—Isaiah 38:18–19 (NASB)

According to Scripture, the only thing that cannot praise God is death! This truth was also exhaled in Psalm 6:5: *"For there is no mention of thee in death; in Sheol who will give thee thanks?"* So unless you are dead, you are expected to faithfully praise God at all times and in all things by using your own lips and your very existence. With all of the things you are experiencing in life, you are expected to give God praise and thanksgiving. This is true even when you are facing hardship, because God said that He inhabits the praises of His people. Therefore, like it says in Matthew 11:25, you must come to the decision that *"I praise Thee, O Father,"* because God our heavenly Father is expecting you as His child, along with all of creation, to have a desire in your heart to praise God on your own.

This portion of the Master Chef's meal has been prepared for believers to share with all those who are not saved because they have no faith in Christ Jesus. You must be born again in order to enjoy the blessings that have been prepared for all of the King's kids.

Sin has separated the sinner from the King, the God who created us, and the only way back to Him is to go through His Son, Jesus Christ, who returned to earth to save you and me. It is time for the unsaved to stop dining with Satan, the devil, by feeding off the lies that they have believed and received, and to start dining with the King by feasting on the Living Word of Truth. However, in order to dine at the King's banquet table, everyone must receive God's invitation by accepting the Son of God, Jesus Christ, as their personal Lord and Savior. God has a wonderful plan for every life, because Jesus wants to present you with praise to God the Father.

If you desire to experience the full and meaningful abundance of life by inheriting all the promises and blessings given

WHY ARE YOU WAITING TO EXHALE
When Everything that Has Breath Is Required to Praise the Lord?

to every child of God, then you must surrender your will and turn your life over the King. You can do this by faith as you repeat this simple prayer below.

If you are already saved, please spend a few moments to share this prayer with those outside the kingdom of God so they too will be filled with the Aged Royal Wine of the Holy Spirit and be covered by the blood of Christ so they can receive a blessing for eternity. However, if you seek the blessing of the Lord for Him to save you, then you can repeat the following prayer, and the God of this universe will rejoice in praise to exalt you and receive you as His own possession. He desires to bless you and lift you up in praise.

THE PRAYER OF PRAISE

"Lord, I need You. Thank You for dying on the cross for my sins. Please forgive me. I open the door to my heart and receive You as my personal Lord and Savior. Thank You for forgiving me of my sins and giving me eternal life. Now take control of my life and make me the kind of person you want me to be. In Jesus's name I pray, Amen."

If you have prayed this prayer to be saved, praise God, because you are now born again, and God now considers you one of His adopted children in the family of God. I encourage you, as a new believer in Christ, to continue praying and reading the Bible every day. Ask God to lead you to a Bible-teaching church where you can be surrounded by your newly adopted brothers and sisters in Christ and grow into a strong and healthy Christian as you praise God with your new life.

The King and all of His children rejoice and welcome our newly adopted brother or sister in Christ into the holy family of God. Now that you are in this holy family, please take a seat at the spiritual banquet table of the King, praise God, and dine on the Word of God until your heart is content.

Welcome to the family, and God bless you, sweet prince or princess!

LONG LIVE THE KING OF OUR SALVATION!

PRAISE GOD, EVERYBODY!

§

REMEMBER SAINTS

With every situation, circumstance, trial, tribulation, problem or issue; Lift the Name of the LORD and Put a PRAISE with It!

WHY ARE YOU WAITING TO EXHALE
When Everything that Has Breath Is Required to Praise the Lord?

Your Spiritual Gourmet Chef

The Author
of
The Royal Candlelight's
Why Are You Waiting to Exhale?

Lynn Williams is a certified gourmet chef with a culinary arts degree in French cooking. She received her college degree in culinary arts and hotel management. Presently she is attending the Hebrew University of Israel to extend her education and interest in Hebrew Bible course studies. She is the cofounder of The Royal Candlelight Christian Publishing Company. Her career has been established as an author, workshop presenter, Bible study teacher at the Teleois Institute, and ministry director for Vacation Bible School, events planning, Fitly Joined, and the political awareness ministries of Ecclesia Christian Fellowship, one of California's well-known churches in the community and in the Inland Empire, located in San Bernardino, California,

Lynn has owned her catering, floral designing, wedding and events planning business for over thirty years. She has also developed her own line of Christian books called The Royal Candlelight Christian Book Series. This series of books is being developed to point you to the truth, which can only be found in the Word of God. Five of the books will be "spiritual culinary recipe books," study guides written in culinary allegory based on all sixty-six books of the Bible. A second line of Christian books will be based on life experiences and various life situations and social topics of interest, written in allegory to encourage true believers in God by assisting them in finding the truth about what God has to say about their life challenges according to the governing principles of His Word.

Lynn is dedicated to humbly serving God and His people by taking every opportunity to minister, love, and cater to "picking up the broken pieces in the lives of believers."

WHY ARE YOU WAITING TO EXHALE
When Everything that Has Breath Is Required to Praise the Lord?

Share Your Thoughts with The Author

We want to hear from you about this book. Also, if you are interested in Lynn's line of Christian books and want us to contact you on all new releases, please e-mail us at: www.royalcandlelight.com or royal.candlelight@hotmail.com

Other Publications By The Author

30 Minute Meals with God

The Royal Candlelight and You

The Four Seasons of Praise Journal and Study Guide

Royal Candlelight Christian Publishing Company

"Royalty in the Making"

CHRISTIAN AUTHORS INTERESTED IN PUBLISHING

WITH

ROYAL CANDLELIGHT CHRISTIAN PUBLISHING COMPANY

check out our website, email us, or give us a call

(909) 999-2433.

And be blessed!

www.ingramcontent.com/pod-product-compliance
Lightning Source LLC
Chambersburg PA
CBHW042323150426
43192CB00001B/27